# Color the Bible™ 3-in-1

## Artwork by Michal Sparks, Denise Urban, and Marie Michaels

**HARVEST HOUSE PUBLISHERS**
EUGENE, OREGON

*Design and production by Harvest House Publishers, Inc.*

*Cover by Katie Brady Design, Eugene, Oregon*

COLOR THE BIBLE is a registered trademark of The Hawkins Children's LLC. Harvest House Publishers, Inc., is the exclusive licensee of the federally registered trademark COLOR THE BIBLE.

Includes the previously *Color the Psalms*, *Color Your Blessings*, and *Color the Names of God*.

## COLOR THE BIBLE™ 3-IN-1

Copyright © 2016 by Dugan Design Group, Michal Sparks, Denise Urban
Published by Harvest House Publishers
Eugene, Oregon 97402
www.harvesthousepublishers.com

ISBN 978-0-7369-6869-0 (pbk.)

**Printed in the United States of America**

16 17 18 19 20 21 22 23 / VP-JC / 10 9 8 7 6 5 4 3 2 1

# A Good Place to Begin

This coloring book is for artists of all ages and talents, and that means you! Let your creative spirit free, choose any color you like, and make each beautiful image your own. There are no rules except to have fun.

Enjoy the process. Feel free to use colored pencils, pens, watercolors, markers, and crayons—or any combination—to add color and texture to each design. Notice that all the pictures are printed on just one side of the paper. To keep colors from bleeding through to the next page, simply slip an extra piece of paper underneath the page you're working on. When finished, you might like to remove the page from the book, trim it to size, and frame your artwork for all to see.

Most importantly, have fun with the process. Enjoy experimenting with contrasting colors or different shades of the same color. Try lighter hues for a softer look, or layer and blend your colors for even more options. Allow some white space or saturate the entire piece with rich, vibrant color, depending on your mood. Let your worries go, relax in the moment, and allow your creative spirit to lead the way!

# Color the Names of God

### Artwork by Marie Michaels

Elohim

GOD

In the beginning God created the heavens and the earth.

Genesis 1:1

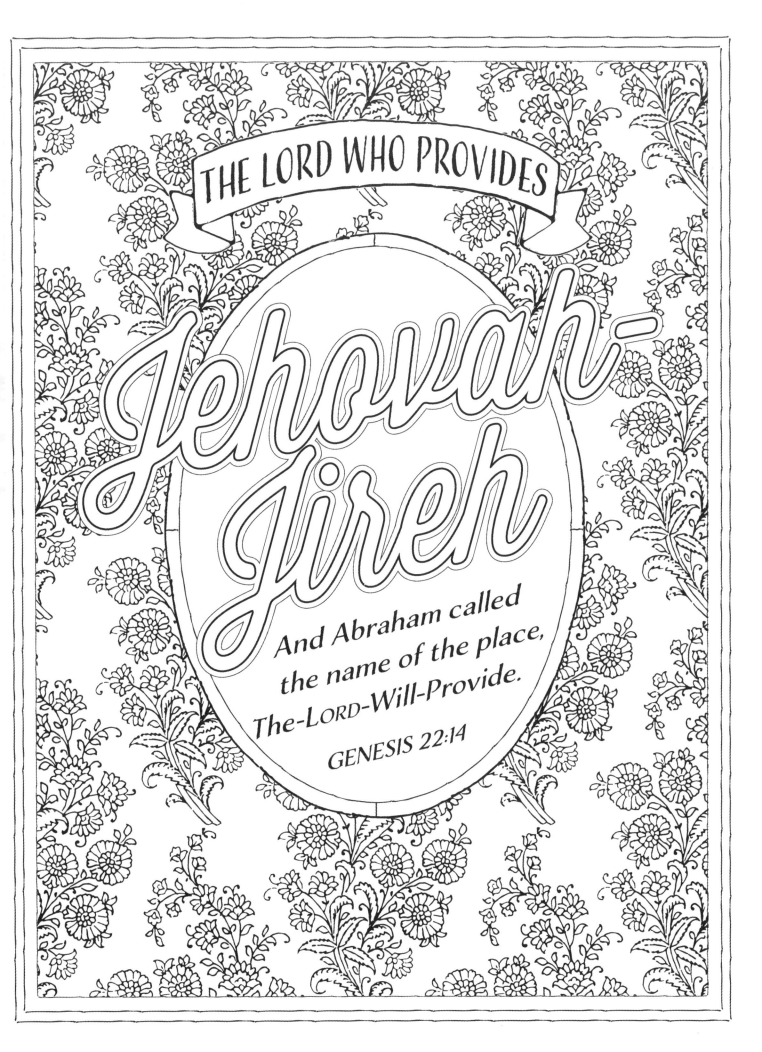

THE LORD WHO PROVIDES

Jehovah-Jireh

And Abraham called
the name of the place,
The-LORD-Will-Provide.

GENESIS 22:14

# El Shaddai
## God Almighty

WHO IS LIKE YOU,
LORD GOD ALMIGHTY?
YOU, LORD, ARE MIGHTY, AND YOUR
FAITHFULNESS SURROUNDS YOU.
PSALM 89:8

Immanuel
GOD WITH US

The Lord himself will give you a sign: The virgin
will conceive and give birth to a son, and will
call him Immanuel.  ISAIAH 7:14

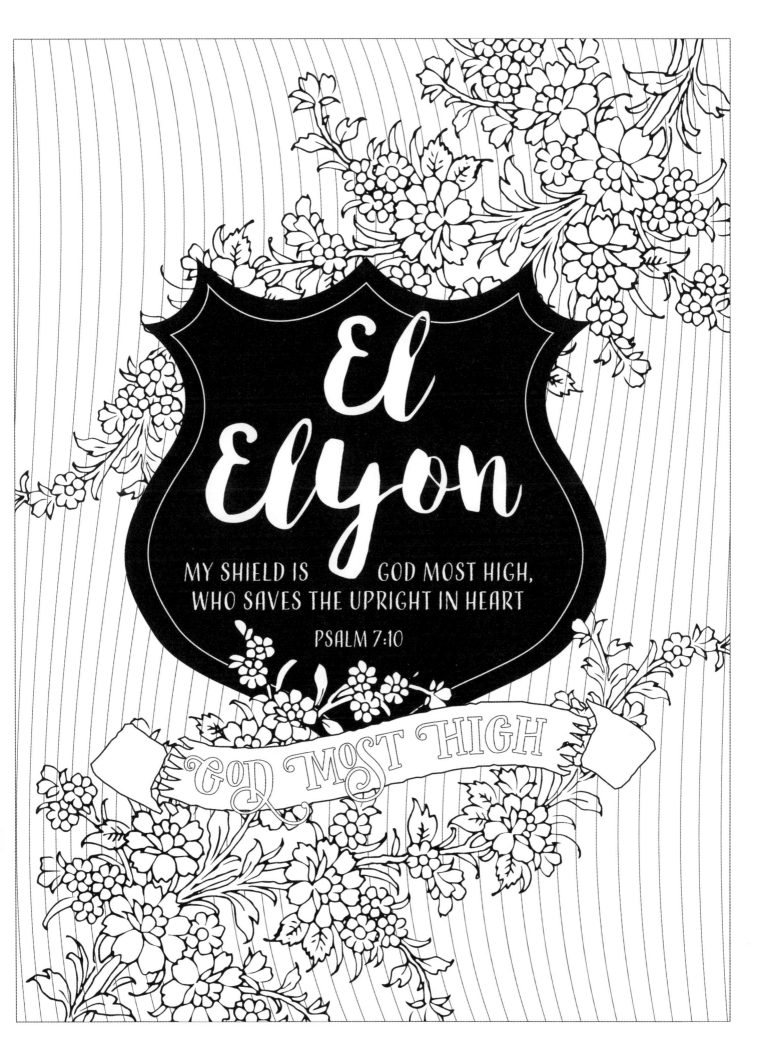

El Roi

The God Who Sees

You are the God who sees me.

Genesis 16:13

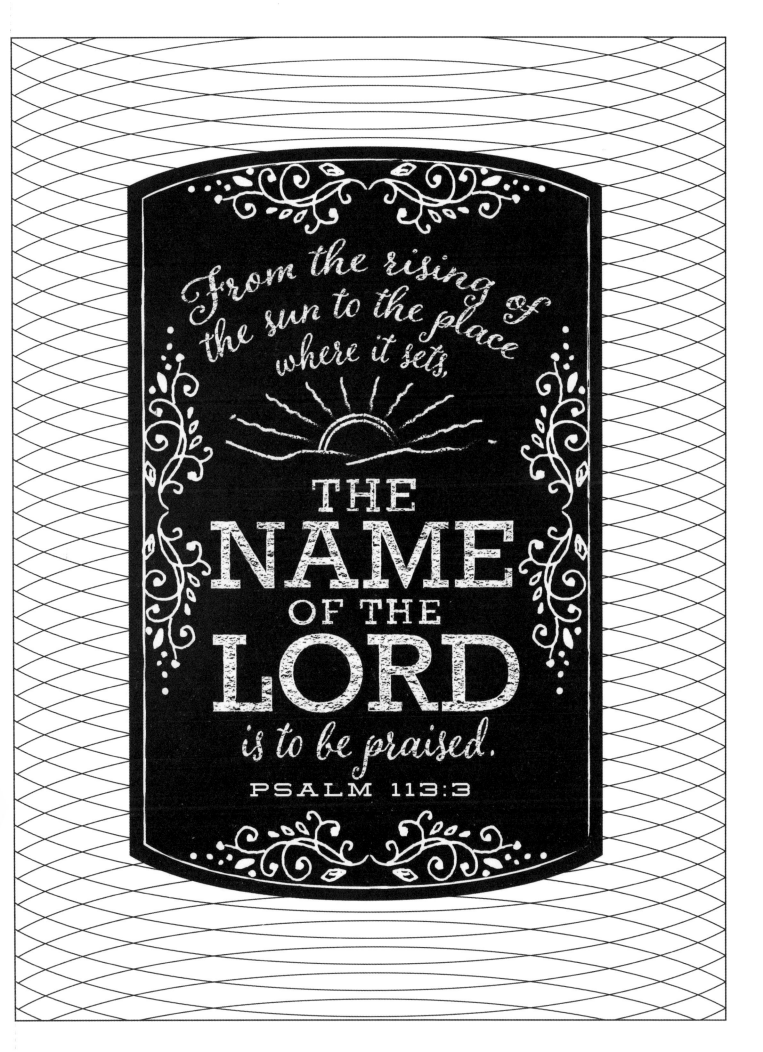

# Jehovah~Shalom

**THE LORD IS PEACE**

Gideon built an altar to the
LORD there and called it
The LORD Is Peace.
JUDGES 6:24

El Olam

The Everlasting God

The LORD is the true God;
He is the living God
and the everlasting King.

Jeremiah 10:10

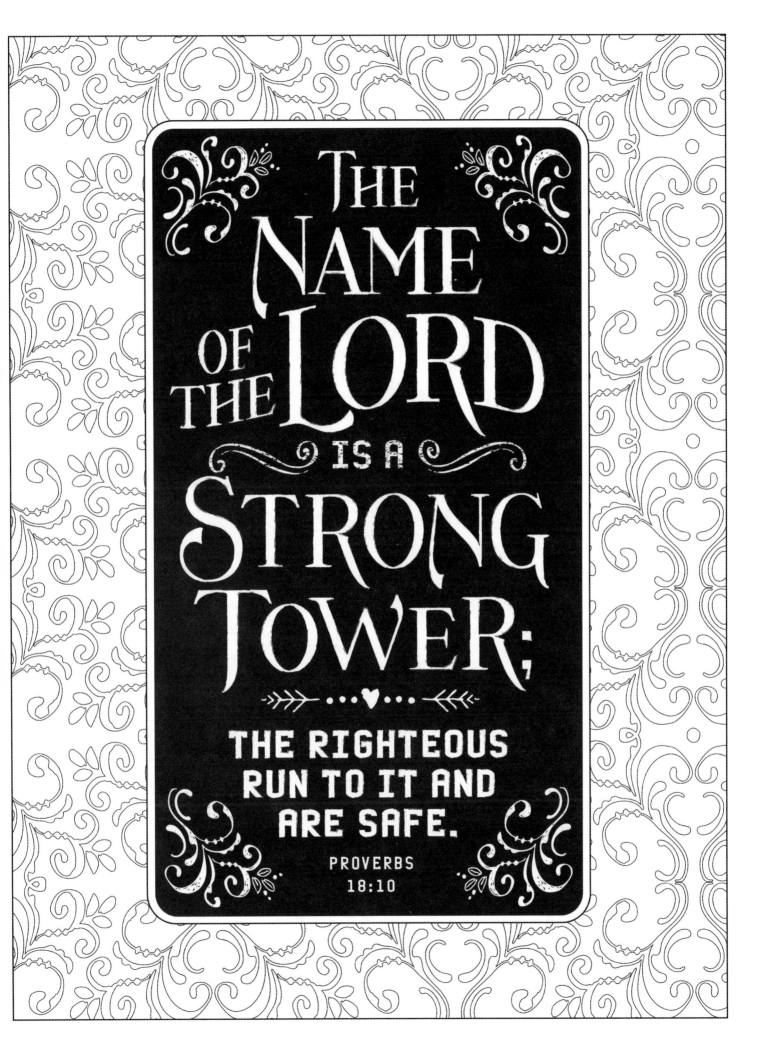

Jehovah-Rapha

THE LORD WHO HEALS

I am the LORD,
who heals you.
Exodus 15:26

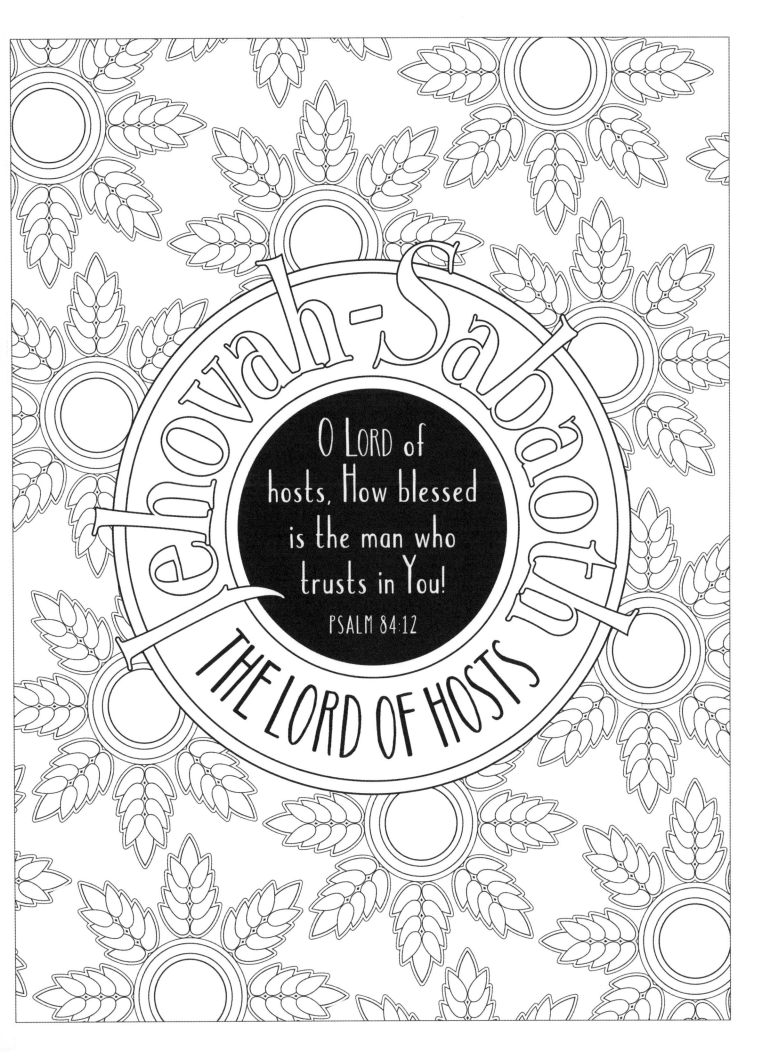

Jehovah-Sabaoth

THE LORD OF HOSTS

O Lord of hosts, How blessed is the man who trusts in You!

PSALM 84:12

JEHOVAH-
MEKODDISHKEM
The Lord Who Makes Holy

KEEP MY DECREES AND FOLLOW THEM.
I AM THE Lord, WHO MAKES YOU HOLY.
LEVITICUS 20:8

Adonai

the fear of the
Lord—that is wisdom.

JOB 28:28

LORD & MASTER

I will praise you, LORD, among the nations; I will sing the praises of your name.

2 SAMUEL 22:50

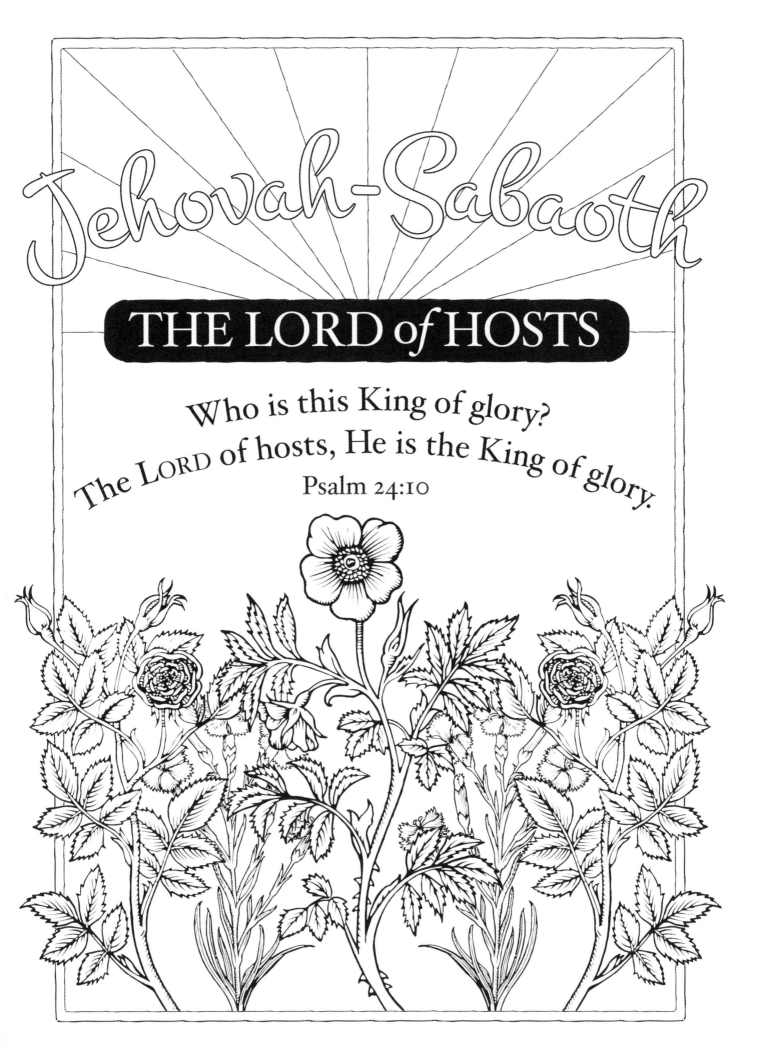

# Jehovah-Sabaoth

## THE LORD of HOSTS

Who is this King of glory?
The LORD of hosts, He is the King of glory.

Psalm 24:10

# Elohim

## GOD

Have mercy on me,
O God, according to
your unfailing love.

PSALM 51:1

Jehovah

LORD

From the
LORD comes
deliverance.
May your
blessing be on
your people.

PSALM 3:8

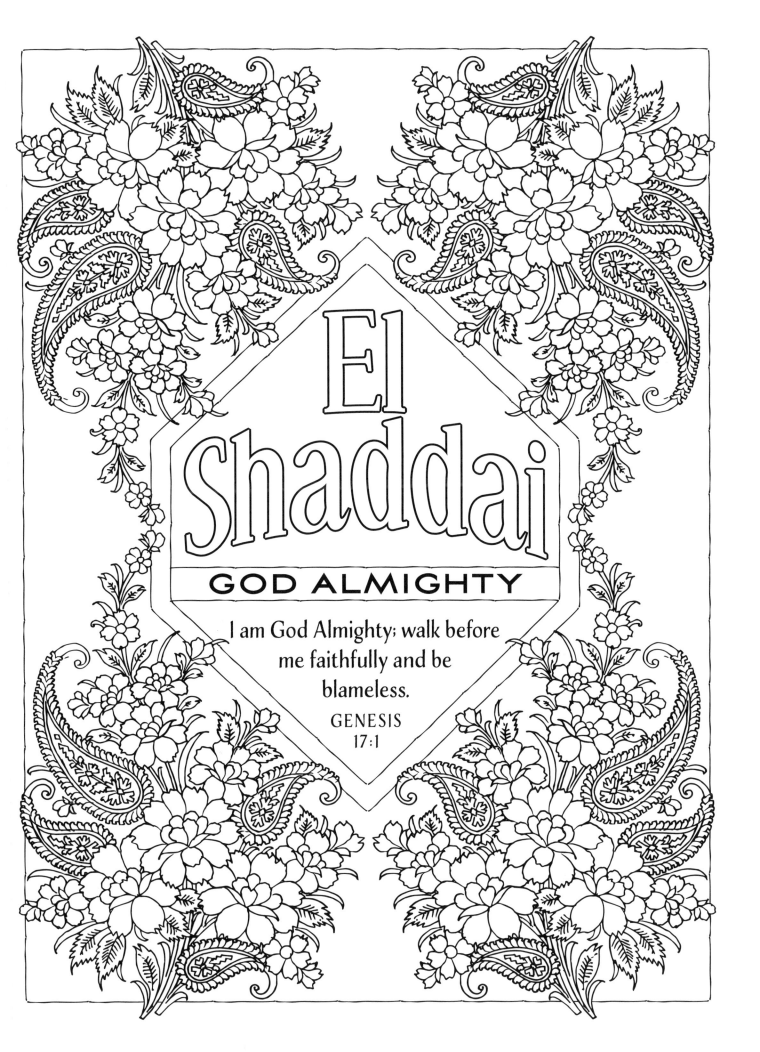

# El Shaddai

## GOD ALMIGHTY

I am God Almighty; walk before
me faithfully and be
blameless.

GENESIS
17:1

Glory In His HOLY NAME; Let the Hearts of Those Who Seek THE LORD Rejoice. LOOK TO THE LORD and Seek HIS FACE Always. 1 Chronicles 16:10-11

# JEHOVAH-NISSI

## The Lord My Banner

Moses built an altar and called its name, The~LORD~Is~My~Banner.

Exodus 17:15

Elohim

GOD

Truly my soul finds rest in God;
my salvation comes from him.

PSALM 62:1

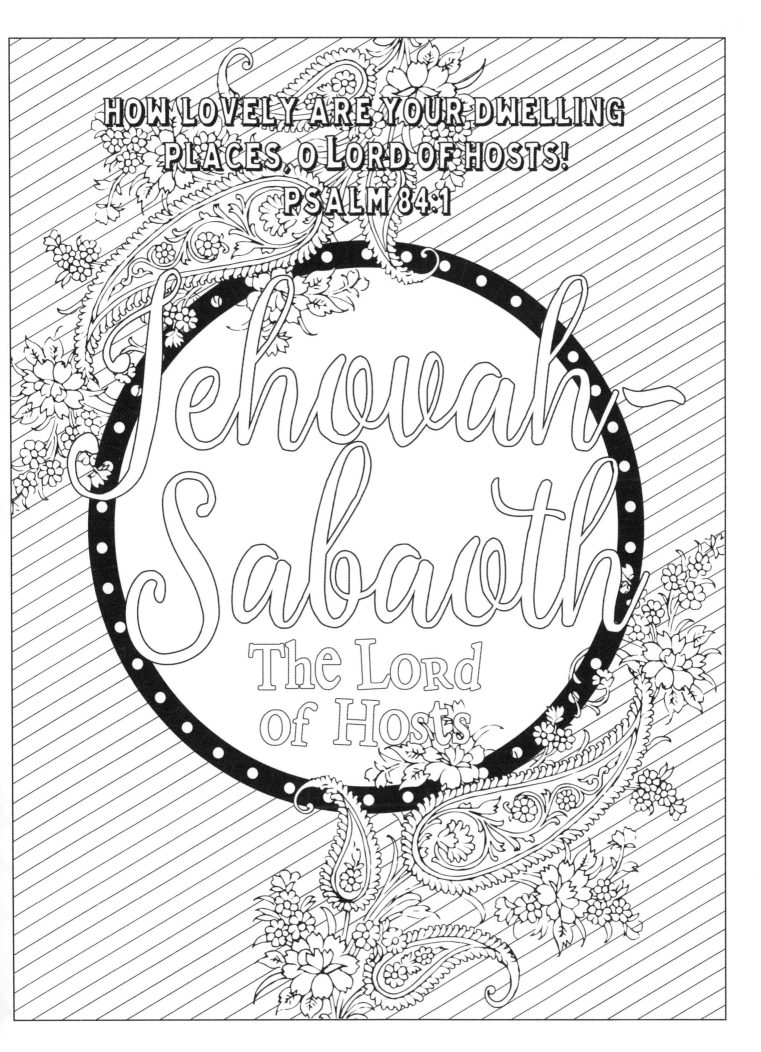

O may Your
glorious name be
blessed & exalted
above all blessing
and praise!

Nehemiah 9:5

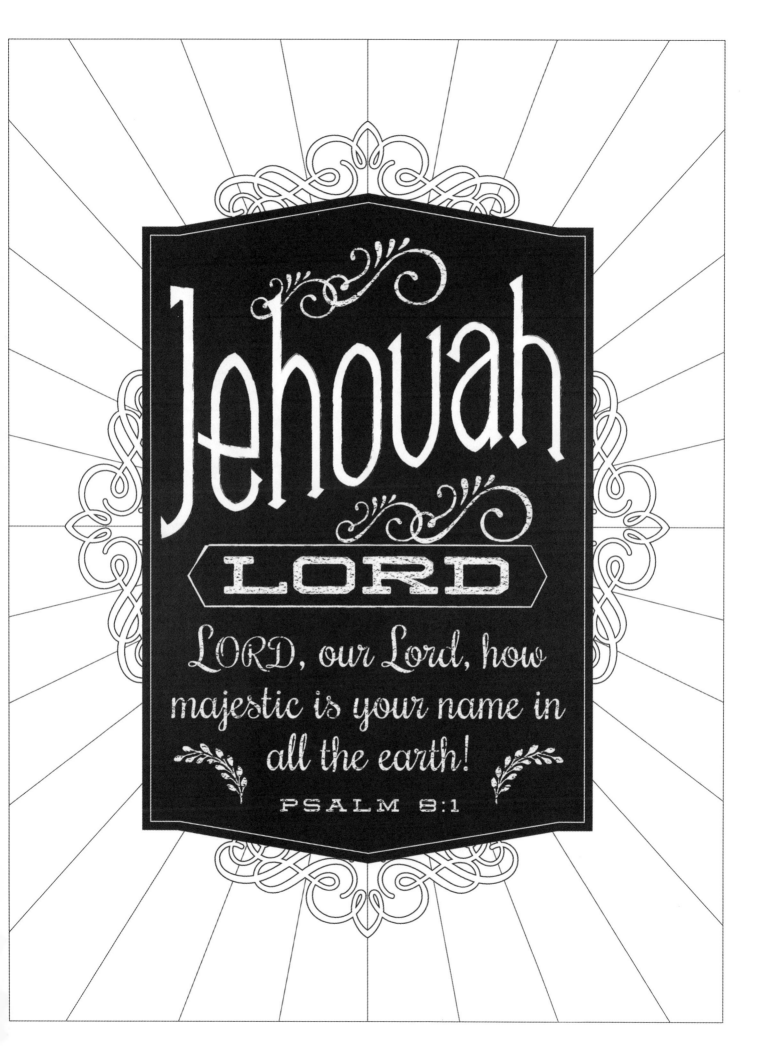

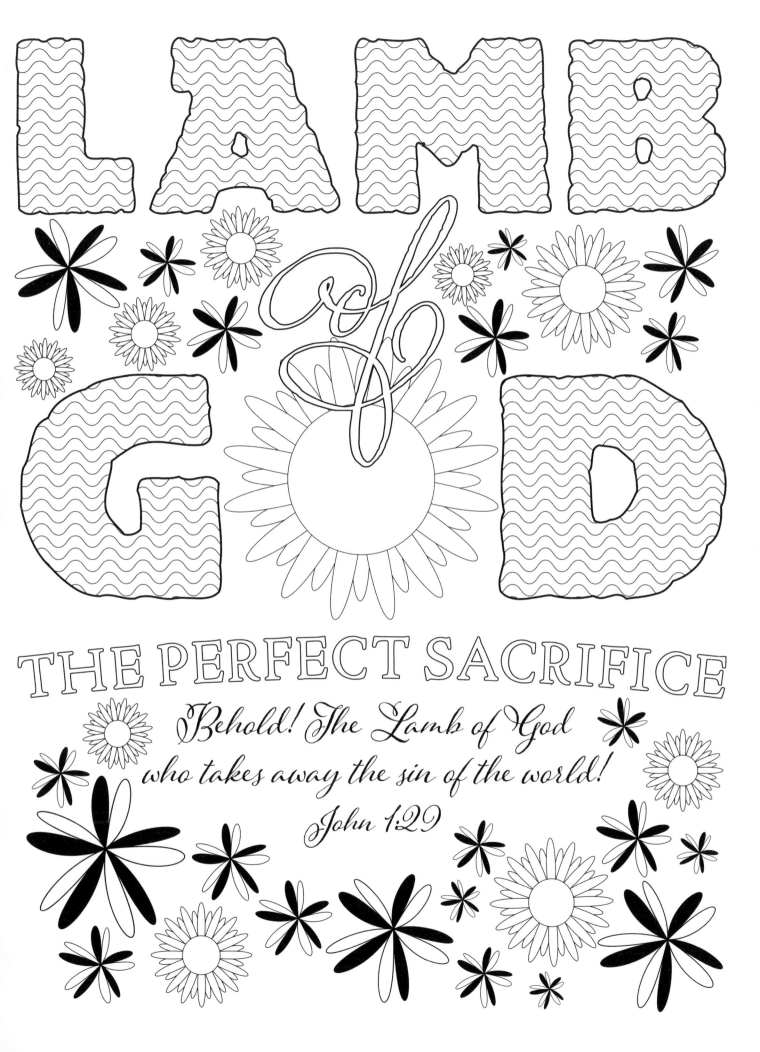

LAMB of GOD

THE PERFECT SACRIFICE

*Behold! The Lamb of God
who takes away the sin of the world!*

*John 1:29*

Those who went ahead and those who followed shouted,

Hosanna!

"Blessed is he who comes in the name of the Lord!"

Mark 11:9

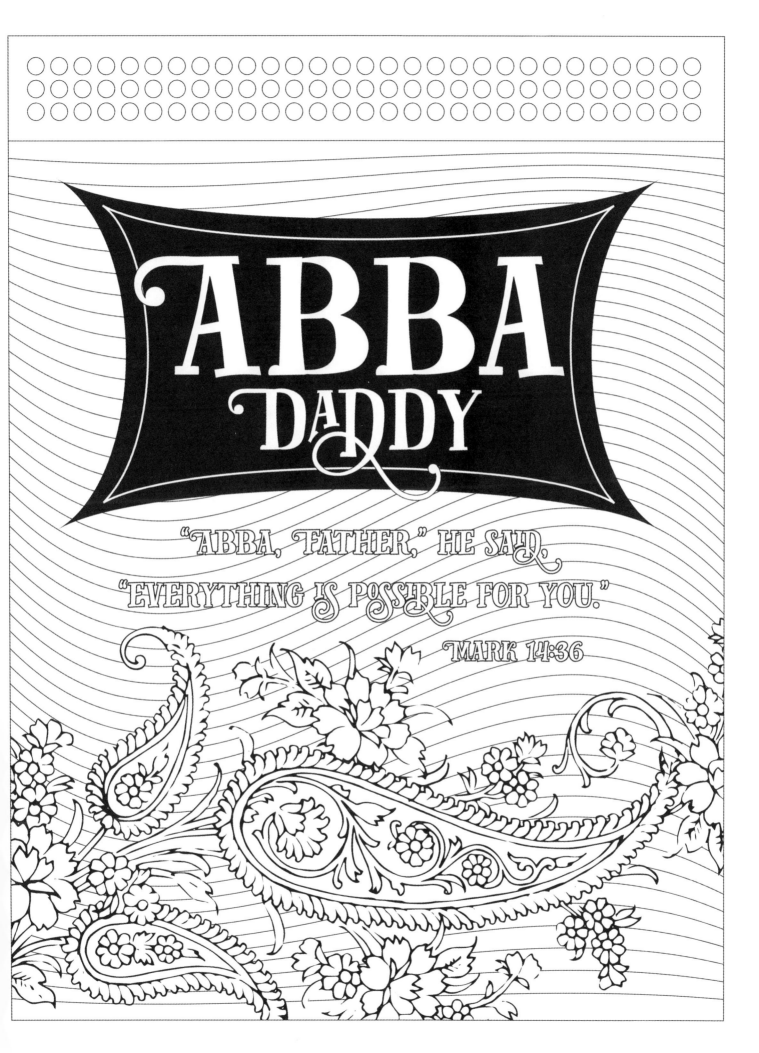

# ABBA DADDY

"ABBA, FATHER," HE SAID,
"EVERYTHING IS POSSIBLE FOR YOU."

MARK 14:36

*A*ND EVERYONE WHO
CALLS ON THE NAME OF
THE LORD WILL BE SAVED.

ACTS 2:21

THEREFORE GOD EXALTED HIM TO THE HIGHEST PLACE AND GAVE HIM THE NAME THAT IS ABOVE EVERY NAME, THAT AT THE NAME OF

JESUS

EVERY KNEE SHOULD BOW, IN HEAVEN AND ON EARTH AND UNDER THE EARTH, AND EVERY TONGUE ACKNOWLEDGE THAT JESUS CHRIST IS LORD, TO THE GLORY OF GOD THE FATHER.

PHILIPPIANS 2:9-11

# Color the Psalms

Artwork by Michal Sparks

You will show me
*the path of life;*
In Your presence is
*fullness of joy;*
At Your right hand are
*pleasures*
*forevermore.*

PSALM 16:11

The Lord has done great things for us.

PSALM 126:3

who lifts up my head. I cried to the Lord with my voice, and He heard me from His holy hill.

You, O Lord, are a shield for me, my glory, and the One

Psalm 3:3-4

The earth is the Lord's,
and all its fullness,
the world and those who
dwell therein.

PSALM 24:1

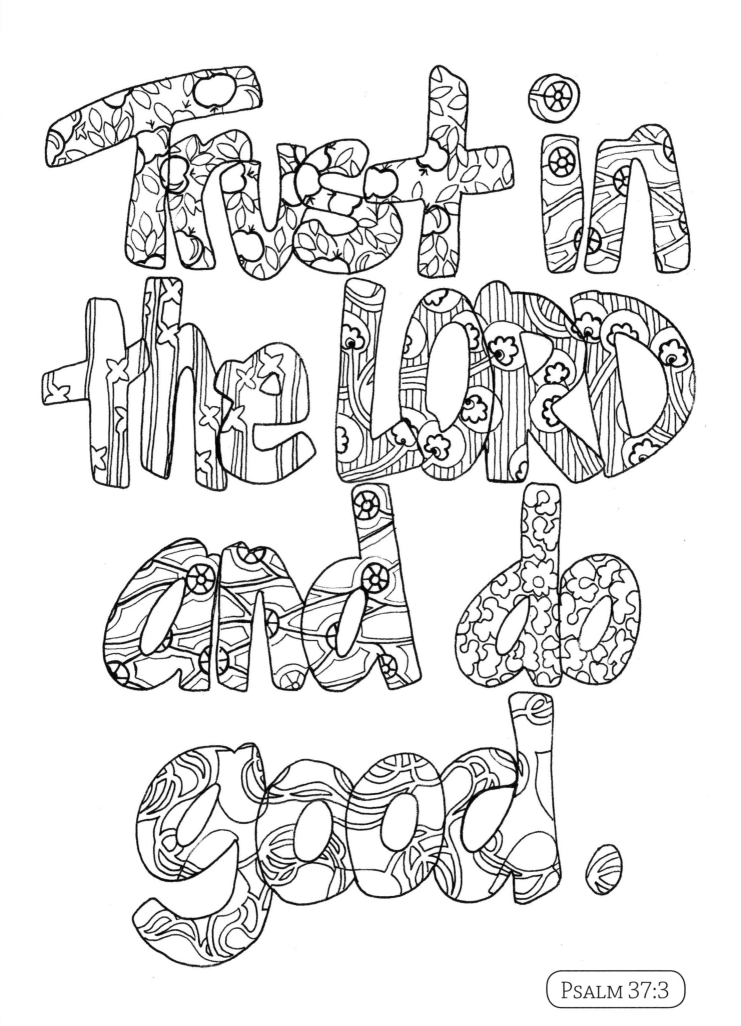

Trust in the Lord and to do good.

PSALM 37:3

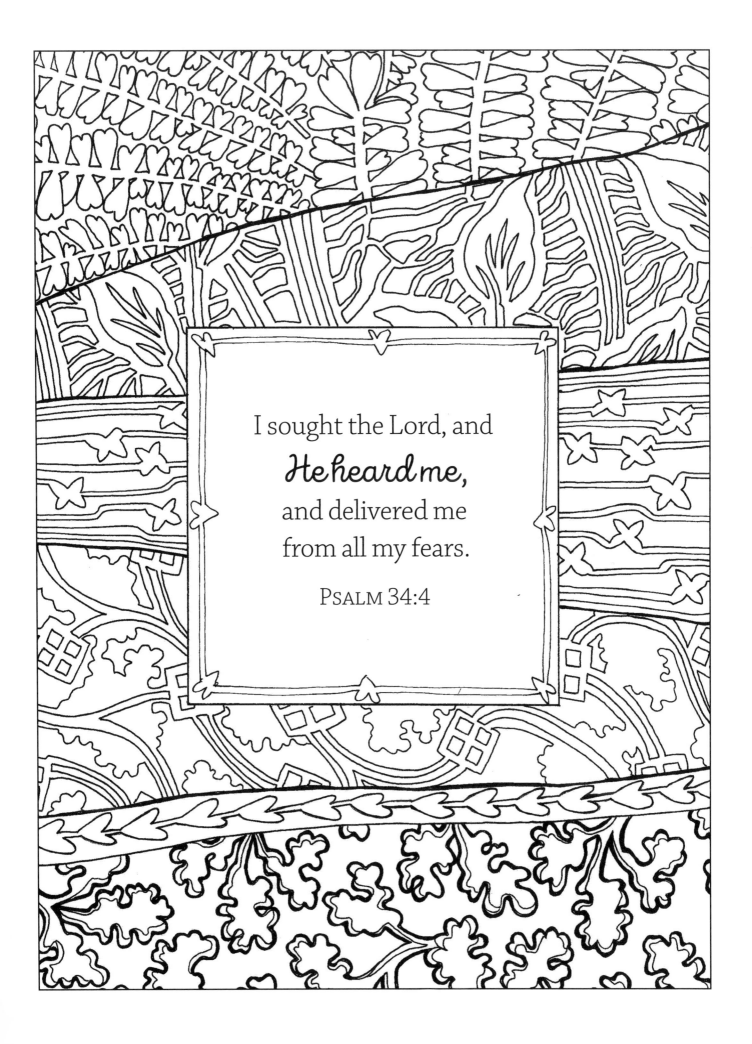

I sought the Lord, and
*He heard me,*
and delivered me
from all my fears.

PSALM 34:4

The Lord is near to those who have a *broken heart*, and saves such as have a *contrite spirit*.

Psalm 34:18

He hears my voice & my prayer for Mercy.

PSALM 116:1

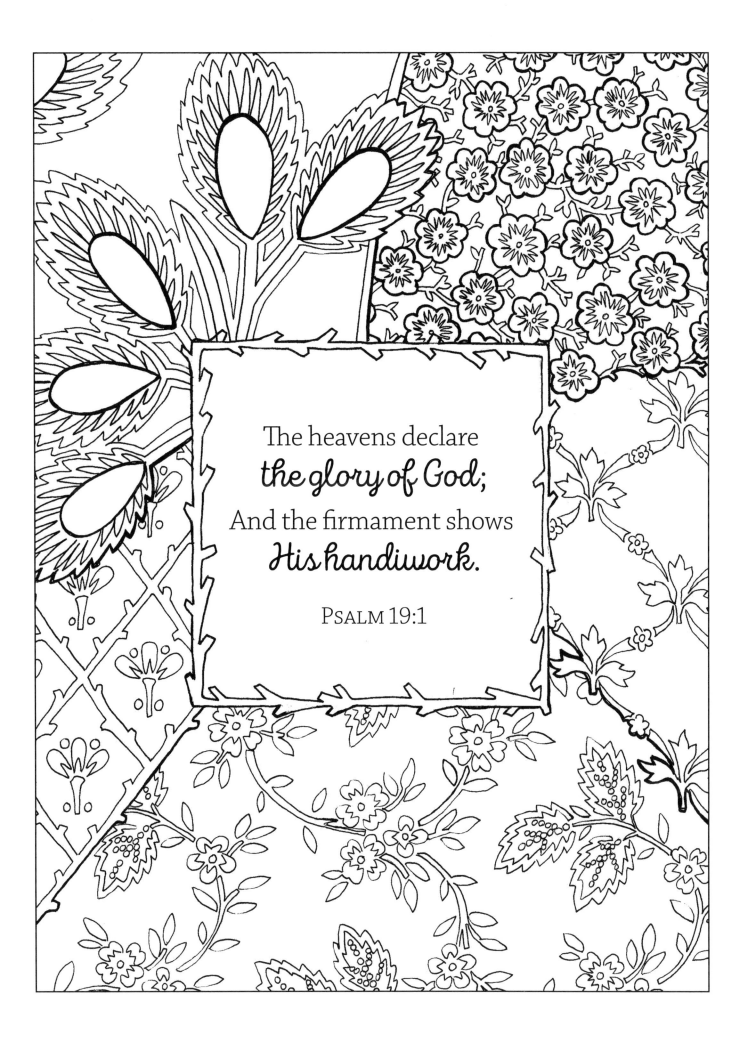

The heavens declare
*the glory of God;*
And the firmament shows
*His handiwork.*

PSALM 19:1

the LORD is my Shepherd

PSALM 23:1

Our help is in the name of the Lord,

who made heaven and earth.

Psalm 124:8

He alone is my rock and my Salvation.

PSALM 62:2

Restore to me the
*joy of Your salvation,*
and uphold me by
Your generous Spirit.

Psalm 51:12

The LORD is my light and my Salvation

PSALM 27:1

mercy shall follow me all the days of my life; And I will dwell in the house of the Lord forever.

My cup runs over. Surely goodness and

PSALM 23:5-6

Delight yourself
also in the Lord,
and He shall give you
the desires of your heart.

PSALM 37:4

Be still and know that I am God

Psalm 46:10

Yea, though I walk
through the valley of
the shadow of death,
*I will fear no evil;*
*For You are with me;*
Your rod and Your staff,
they comfort me.

PSALM 23:4

I lift up my eyes to the hills... my help comes from the Lord.

Psalm 121:1-2

I will praise You,
for I am *fearfully* and
*wonderfully* made;
Marvelous are Your works,
and that my soul
knows very well.

PSALM 139:14

Create a pure ♥ in me O GOD

Psalm 51:10

Do not withhold Your tender mercies from me, O Lord; Let Your lovingkindness and Your truth continually preserve me.

Psalm 40:11

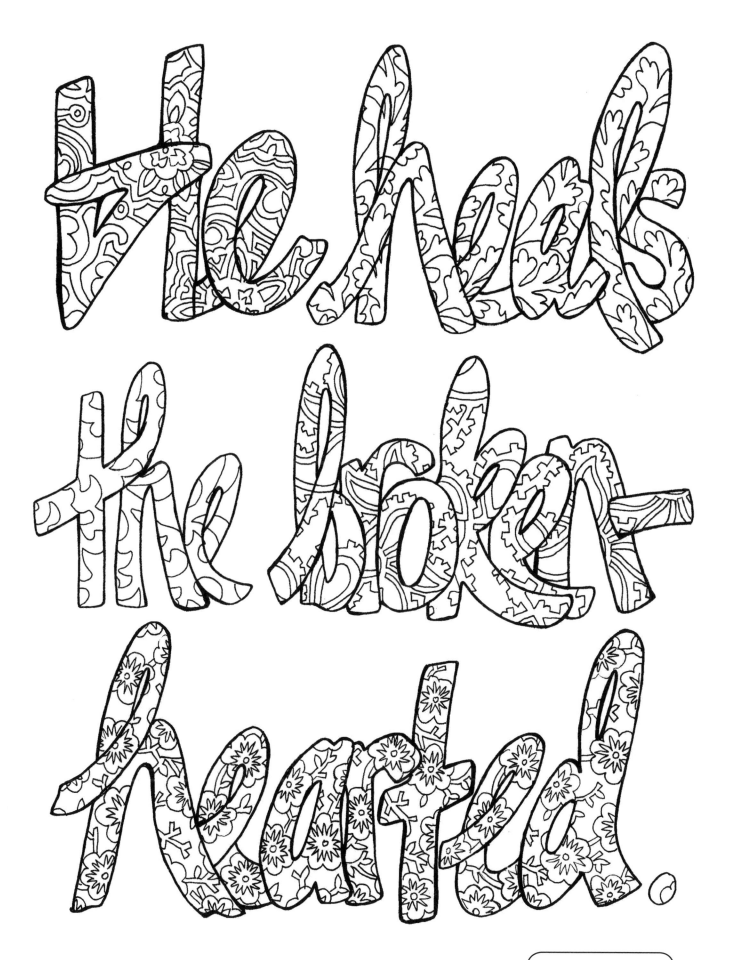

PSALM 147:3

Cast your burden
on the Lord, and
*He shall sustain you;*
He shall never permit
the righteous to be moved.

PSALM 55:22

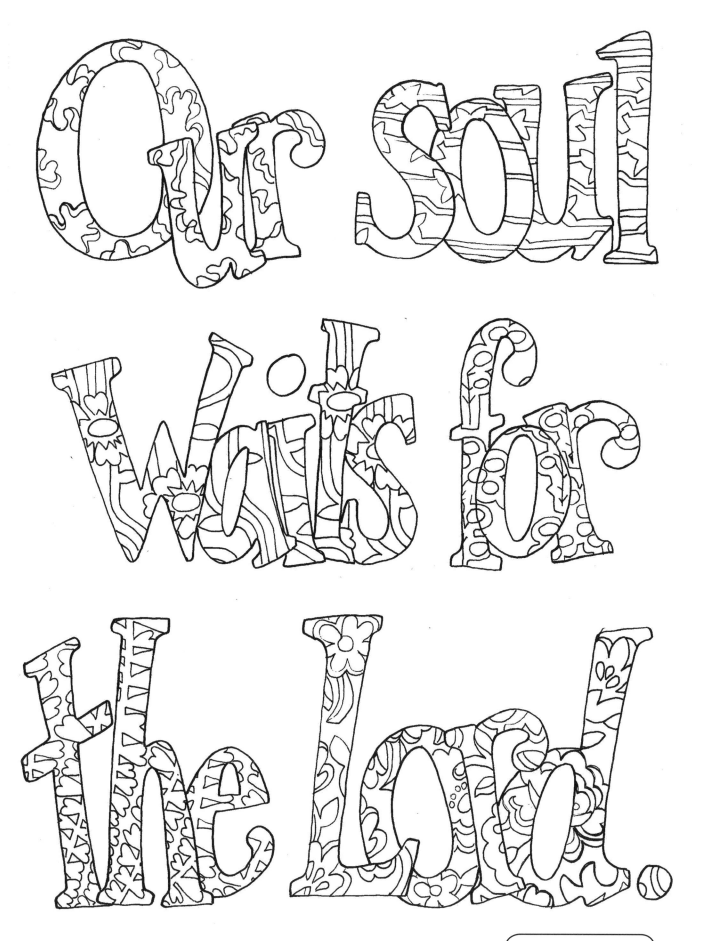

Psalm 33:20

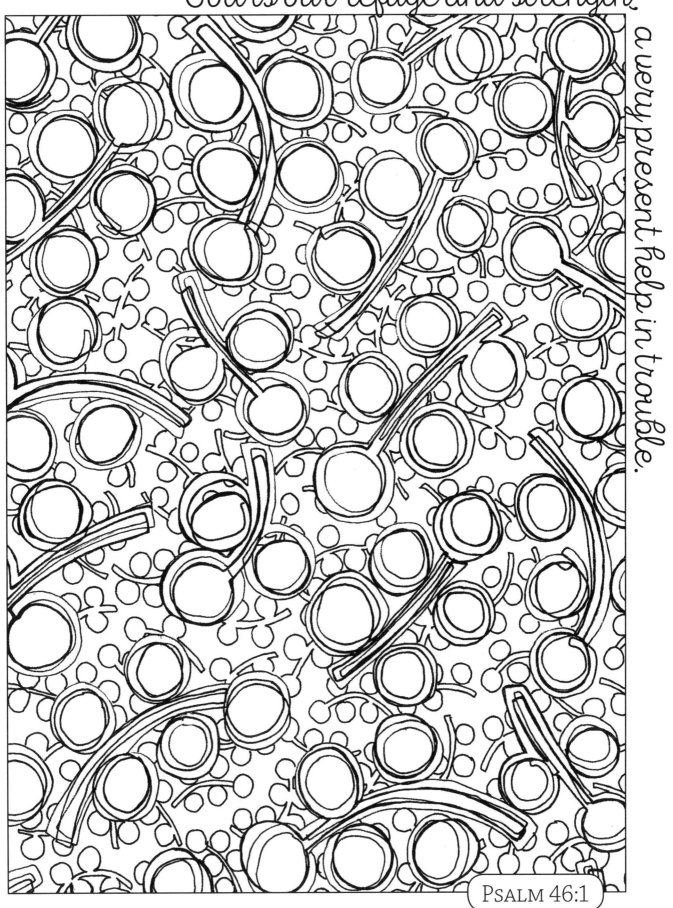

God is our refuge and strength, a very present help in trouble.

Psalm 46:1

When my heart is
overwhelmed;
*Lead me to the rock*
that is higher than I.

Psalm 61:2

Under His wings you shall take refuge.

Psalm 91:4

Give thanks
to the Lord,
*for He is good!*
For His mercy
*endures forever.*

PSALM 107:1

His greatness is unsearchable. One generation shall praise Your works to another. Great is the Lord, and greatly to be praised; And

Psalm 145:3-4

O Lord, my Strength & my Redeemer.

Psalm 19:14

will give grace and glory; No good thing will

For the Lord God is a sun and shield; the Lord

He withhold from those who walk uprightly.

Psalm 84:11

Artwork by Denise Urban

**BLESSED** IS SHE WHO HAS BELIEVED THAT THE LORD WOULD FULFILL HIS PROMISES TO HER! LUKE 1:45

And my God will meet all your needs according to the riches of his glory in Christ Jesus.

Philippians 4:19

Commit to the Lord whatever you do, and he will establish your plans.
PROVERBS 16:3

Every good
and perfect gift
is from above,
coming down from the Father
of the heavenly lights,
who does not change
like shifting shadows.

**JAMES 1:17**

Fear not, for i am with you;
Be not dismayed, for i am your God.
i will strengthen you,
Yes, i will help you.
i will uphold you with my
righteous right hand.

isaiah 41:10

May he give you the desire of your heart and make all your plans succeed.

**PSALM 20:4**

Rejoice in the Lord
always.
I will say it again:
Rejoice!

PHILIPPIANS 4:4

In all things GOD works for the GOOD of those who LOVE him, who have been CALLED according to his PURPOSE.

ROMANS 8:28

Do not be anxious about anything, but in every situation, by prayer and petition, with thanksgiving, present your requests to God.

PHILIPPIANS 4:6

The Lord is faithful to all his promises and loving toward all he has made.

PSALM 145:13

With man this
is imPossible, but
With GOD
All things
Are
Possible!
matthew 19:26

Taste and see
that the Lord is good;
blessed is the one who
takes refuge in him.

PSALM 34:8

Jesus Christ is the same yesterday and today and forever.

HEBREWS 13:8

Love always protects, always trusts, always hopes, always perseveres. Love never fails.
1 Corinthians 13:7-8

The lines have fallen for me in pleasant places; indeed, i have a beautiful inheritance.

PSALM 16:6

The Lord watches over you–the Lord is your shade at your right hand; the sun will not harm you by day, nor the moon by night.

Psalm 121: 5-6

GIVE THANKS TO THE LORD, FOR HE IS GOOD; HIS LOVE ENDURES FOREVER.

1 CHRONICLES 16:34

Commit to the Lord whatever You do, and he will establish Your Plans.

Proverbs 16:3

Salvation belongs to the Lord; your blessing be on Your people!

PSALM 3:8

Praise be to the God and Father of our Lord Jesus Christ, who has blessed us in the heavenly realms with every spiritual blessing in Christ.

EPHESIANS 1:3

The Lord bless you and keep you;
the Lord make his face shine on you
and be gracious to you;
the Lord turn his face toward you
and give you peace.

NUMBERS 6:24-26

**Marie Michaels** represents the combined work of three artists from Dugan Design Group in Minneapolis, Minnesota: Nicole Wallace, Chris Dugan, and Terry Dugan. Their primary creative work is book cover and book interior design, increasingly focused on original content via illustration, photography, and digital media.

**Michal Sparks'** artwork can be found throughout the home-furnishings industry in textiles, gift items, dinnerware, and more. She is the artist for *Words of Comfort for Times of Loss* and *When Someone You Love Has Cancer*. She and her family live in New Jersey.

**Denise Urban** is formally educated in art history, design, and merchandising and is the principal and creative director of UrbanDigits. Her designs and illustrations have appeared in numerous newspapers and magazines throughout the US, and her licensed products can be found in retail stores, such as Kohl's, Target, Walmart, Lowe's, and HomeGoods.

We'd love to see your creations!
Share your finished projects on social media with the hashtag

# #colorthebible

We'll be looking for your artwork!

For information on more
Harvest House coloring books for adults, please visit
**www.harvesthousepublishers.com**